Letting Rain Have Its Say

Letting Rain Have Its Say

Poems by

Donna Baier Stein

Kelsay Books

Cover: "Watering" by Budi Satria Kwan, www.budikwan.com, and cover design by Tom Schneider, www.tomschneiderarts.com

ISBN: 13-978-1-947465-40-4

Kelsay Books
Aldrich Press
www.kelsaybooks.com

Dedicated to my beloved mother, Dorothy Baier

Acknowledgments

The author gratefully acknowledges the journals and anthologies in which some of these poems first appeared.

"Cover-ups" won Third Prize in the 2015 Allen Ginsberg Poetry Awards. "You Asked What Sustains Me" won an Honorable Mention in the 2013 Allen Ginsberg Poetry Awards. "Chez Daisy" won a prize from the Virginia Poetry Council. "News Item from 9/11" as "Comfort Zone" and "Fishing with My Father" were nominated for Pushcart Prizes. Some of these poems also appeared in my 2012 chapbook *Sometimes You Sense the Difference* from Finishing Line Press.

The Beloit Poetry Journal: "Watchman of the Night"
The Caribbean Writer: "At Dawn Beach," "Labour Day, Sint Maarten," and "Wooing Lady Luck in Philipsburg"
Carolina Quarterly: "La Secheresse"
Edison Literary Review: "Staring at a Painting" as "The Visit"
Enchanted Verse: "Trapeze"
Exit 13: "La Secheresse" reprint
Hampden-Sydney Poetry Review: "On My Father's 70th Birthday"
Kansas Quarterly: "Between Seasons" and "Sometimes You Sense the Difference"
Kansas City Outloud (anthology): "Easy Marks"
Life and Legends: "The Orphanage at St. John the Baptist Retreat Center" and "The Cave of the World Is Waiting to Be Lit"
Lips: "At My Mother-in-Law's Funeral" and "Remembering Mark Strand"
The Literary Review: "Travelling on Business, a New Mother" as "It Could Be Sarah," and "News Item after 9/11" as "Comfort Zone"
Many Mountains Moving: "The Frog Prince"
Men & Women: Together & Alone (anthology): "Wooing Lady Luck in Philipsburg"

Midwest Quarterly: "Landslide"

Notre Dame Review: First section of "Etruscan Tomb Paintings" as "Iphigenia"

Paterson Literary Review: "Hospital," "You Asked What Sustains Me," and "Cover-ups"

Phoebe: The George Mason Review: "Cross-stitch" and "Tricks My Aunt Ruth Taught Me" as "Hard Winter"

Pirene's Fountain: "This Meditation" and "Roget's Thesaurus"

The Poet's Domain: "Fortune's Fancy," "I Marry, We Buy a Cabin" as "Apples, Rappahannock County"

Poet Lore: "Leonidion"

Prime Number Magazine: "Fishing with My Father"

RE:AL: The Journal of Liberal Arts: Second section of "Etruscan Tomb Paintings" as "At the Tomb of the Baron." and "First Winter in Lexington"

Soundings East: "Yellow Brick Road"

Sou'wester: "Chasing Down the Dream"

The Spoon River Review: "Even His Red Heart" as "Fishing"

The Stillwater Review: "Conversation"

Verse-Virtual: "The Frog King," "Watchman of the Night," "King Kong," "Iphigenia," and "Carousel" as "Glen Echo"

The Washingtonian: "Glen Echo" and "Still Life at the National Archives"

Contents

III This Meditation

The rain began again. It fell heavily, easily, with no meaning or intention but the fulfillment of its own nature, which was to fall and fall.

—Helen Garner

The way that you remember your life, it's never linear. You have flashes of different moments of your life, and the flashes aren't equal; they have different styles.

—Marjane Satrapi

... you could easily argue that the past, the present, and the future all occur simultaneously.

—Tommy Lee Jones

I For We Are Kin

It is not the level of prosperity that makes for happiness but the kinship of heart to heart and the way we look at the world.

—Alexander Solzhenitsyn

For We Are Kin

On good days, it could have been Copland:
proud boots danced and inverted petticoat tulips
swirled on a Midwestern stage.
Big suns, big moons, land.

Off-stage, hurried as the passing decades,
a gray highway poured across Kansas
like a saxophone's languid tones: smooth
and always heading somewhere.

Days passed, identical as cornstalks in a field.
Amidst those slender stalks I now see
four strong women: my great-grandmother,
grandmother, mother, and me.

The first was a keeper of bees, baker of pies,
cook for two dozen hungry farmhands.
The second, wooed under a clothesline
of clean-flying sheets, became a fresh widow at forty.

Then Mama, whose dream-embroidered bodice
I nuzzled and longed for until one day
I followed the hum of telephone wires
strung between tall poles, pulling me east.

The land rose above a flat plain.
The fields crowded with unfamiliar faces.
As I travelled I whispered:

Women, draw near to me.
Stand at my side, sturdy as silos,
resilient as summer wheat, fruitful as loam.

Draw near, for we are kin.
Cross-bred but kin, we hurl each fertile seed
of faith and song into sky's blue bowl.

Cross-stitch

Their arms fold in like an angel's collapsed wings.
Eyes dart from one tidy square of muslin to another.
The silver needle dives, pulling threads of stories
until it spots safe landing amidst this sampler's red schoolhouses,
brown cows, black buckets, gold baskets of fruit, women
in safe triangle skirts, men in stove-pipe hats,
and silent, straight-lipped children.

The artist's signature fades while her bones
loosen beneath a headstone's epitaph:
Beloved Mother and Wife.

These women focused on one small, intense arena
—for pleasure, duty, or relief.
Like children, they too were silent,
keeping their hands near the occasional red heart,
their eyes mindfully on the work at hand.

Tricks Aunt Ruth Taught Me

Cast a careful eye about you—
look at the size of muskrat houses,
the depth of carrots sounding the soil.

These are tricks worth learning at any age:
how to test the fur on the bottom of a rabbit's foot
or the skin on a potato. If the fur's thick
or the skin tough, expect a hard winter.

Then toss the almanac over your shoulder
and ignore weather maps on TV,
because these are the signs to look for:

Cows' hooves breaking off early.
Worms crawling into abandoned houses.
Screech owls beginning to sound,
to your ears, like women crying.

Edith Rose Hinote

In my great grandmother's kitchen
with its wood-burning range,
scored oak table, and square ochre tiles,
she fed hungry farm hands
steaming drop biscuits, honeycomb from her bees,
ham and mustard beans, candied dills, raisin pie.

She dried corn in cloth sugar sacks;
boiled eggs from her Rhode Island whites;
wove rugs of burlap; stitched quilt patterns
like Dakota Star, Queen's Delight, Bird's Eye View.

She made soap in the butchering kettle
and red pepper tea to cure chicken cholera.

Whatever grief was in her life crouched silent
behind a hard face above a hand-crocheted collar.
Her hair curled tight as Brillo.

At 83, she shared strong coffee
each morning with her neighbor,
the widowed Mrs. Doakes,
until one morning, pulling pie from the oven,
she slipped to the ochre tiles, spirit rising
warm, fragrant, formless as steam.

Don't Listen to Me

when it comes to
searching the heart
for memories of childhood.

Don't trust any imperfect tales
of a tall, bespectacled father
running under a swing
at a park in Burlington, Iowa,
pushing it high so
my black and white saddle shoes
scraped an impossible sky.

Don't imagine that
a Midwestern childhood
can be anything other
than perfect, or that Fair Acres Drive
won't later become another Eden
always tempting you out of your current life.

Don't let me forget
how the swing's leather seat cradled me,
how my small hands clutched the metal chains,
how the peppermint-striped eyeglasses
I'd worn since age three
arced like the wings of an angel.

Still Life at the National Archives

In a basement in our nation's capital,
a microfilm reader hums, bringing
my Grandmother's childhood town
to life, reborn as she bends
to the flickering light.

Her crooked finger strokes
the screen, names still remembered:
Ada Jessup, Reuben and Otis Yoder,
even Sherman Zook: census taker, apiarist, friend.

The years collide as we travel
back to 1910, East Lynne Township, Missouri.

Grandma was nine and rode with her mother
beyond the edge of town, beyond midnight,
to see the light that had been promised.
It was April, and word was Halley's comet
would come closer than ever to earth.

It's easy to imagine her finger,
then smooth and straight,
pointing up at the black sky canvas,
the buggy wheels stopping,
eager for the mystery still to come.

Fishing with My Father

In Colorado, at Call of the Canyon,
we fished for rainbow trout
which my Grandma would
skin and debone, bread and fry
in a cast iron skillet.

When my father dies,
I want to take him back
to those sweet-rushing streams,
so his ashes can mix with the
clear water pouring over
smooth rocks in the channel.

And just as a stream
sometimes overflows its banks,
my father, in his future form,
will leave the edges of
his skin and swim elsewhere.

I want to return to the log cabin,
light a kerosene lamp,
read an *Alfred Hitchock Mystery Magazine*,
pray hard enough to bring my young father
back to me, just like he was, forever.

I want the waters to wash over me, too,
to hear their rock-borne music endlessly
so that the stuff we are made of
tumbles in the water's easy flow,
each cell a fish-shaped flash
of silvery blue green with broad red stripe,
slipping through the current,
teasing the hook and line of my heart.

The Lull

Fogbound, I imagined
our child asleep in his room,
the prayer-bent head of a parakeet,
my book still open, unread.

I rise, walk into the baby's room,
see what may be the hand of God
in a land where dinosaurs romp
in blue and green among blond curls
splayed on an impressionable pillow.

Father & Son in the Plot Device of Dream World

Waking, I snare last night's dream:
my father halving a goldfish in his teeth
while a second, veil-tailed, swims in a glass bowl,
its saffron form almost transparent
and recoiling from the stubborn boundaries of its realm.

> *Carp: a fish originally found in China;*
> *also to find fault, cavil.*

This one's a garibaldi, a brilliant damselfish.
I think of gold, then goldstone, of the mica
I found in Cripple Creek,
and suddenly recall another dream
where a man has shot me in the foot.

Crippled. The line catches as I reel in
other images from last night's pool:
my son climbing a hard-backed tortoise,
its carapace mottled brown and yellow.

> *Tortoise: from the Latin tort,*
> *so-called from its crooked feet.*

It's never just a turtle but the beginning,
the foundation, of all things.
Rising from its watery pool,
this one locks limpid eyes on mine,
says "Don't let go!"

All of them are with me—
fish, tortoise, man, boy—
in morning air or midnight dream,

passing between the elements,
pushing against the edges of our selves,
freer than we could have imagined.

Carousel

Installed at Glen Echo Park in 1921 (the canopy and the carved figures were made by the Dentzel Carousel Company of Germantown, Pennsylvania) glenechopark.org

Turning, I harness an image
of my two-year-old son
in the canopied mirror
peeling above our heads.
I see the mirror-image of his horse
painted rose, brown, blue, oyster-white.

A thousand lights sparkle
around our reflections.

As the carousel circles,
we pass a man whittling
a full-maned and burly lion.
He stands mute near the Wurlitzer organ,
spilling out notes from
viola, flageolet, piccolo, and bass.

I imagine
the next time
my hair will be white,
my son a grown man.

In that hypnotic pool
of images, the years quicken.
As we dismount, we tilt
on warped floorboards,
lean on a far-sighted giraffe
to find footing in what
appears to be now.

II Wooing Lady Luck

There be three things which are too wonderful for me, yea, four which I know not: The way of a eagle in the air; the way of a serpent upon a rock; the way of a ship in the midst of the sea; and the way of a man with a maid.

—Proverbs XXX, v. 18-19

I Travel East, Marry, Buy a Cabin

Come spring my new husband and I will move
to a cabin that now lies beyond sight,
planted among hills freckled with cows.
The road will be lined with pink dogwoods
and snake past an old cemetery, grass-shrouded
and dappled with flat markers,
past eagle-eyed Mrs. White's white house,
past the Loves' fishing pond lively with trout.
We will nuzzle into the succor of hills
and grasp the eternal temptation of apples:
the Jonathans, Staymans, and Winesaps.
Rome Beauties, firm and slightly tart.
Biting into one now, I can almost taste
what living in the cabin could be like for us:
delightful, bracing, ever-lasting.

Fortune's Fancy

Fearing loss of luck,
we hung the horseshoe
upside down today.
If only it were so simple!
To follow old traditions,
mimic the movements
of those who came before us
and learn from their lucky tales:
how, with each new home
the settlers built,
after the last nail was pounded
and the final rafter hung,
a horseshoe was hung upside down—
a willing vessel for luck's liquidity.
Now, we sit in the cabin
hoping to contain
our own fortunate moments.
So far, we prosper:
through the screen door
I see mountain laurel
burst into lucky-starred petticoats
like those faithful pioneers once wore.

Letting Rain Have Its Say

We listen to the crickets' shivaree,
the breathless calls of whippoorwill.
We call back: a stereo of thieves
(bird and human voices) echoes
against the walls of the cabin.

We hear the whippoorwill name itself in three syllables.
Imagine him perched on a limb, kin of the nightjar.

Rain taps the tin roof until,
cuddled in half-sleep, we fear
it will wash us away, send
our home down the side of this mountain.

There's something to this—
letting rain have its say,
being carried away, intact.
Later I dream of white tigers and raccoons.

Labour Day, Sint Maarten, First Anniversary

Bars drop down across store doors and
today, the driver tells us,
workers rest and come together.
His two-way radio burbles, *He can't come in.*

In the village we see gingerbread houses
and dark-skinned men
playing cards at square tables,
their faces sacramental in lamplight.

Across the way, a piece of broken latticework
hangs from a door, crazy as a bride's wink.
Goats climb in and out of rusted cars,
and even the hibiscus trees clutch beer bottles.

Wooing Lady Luck

We spent the day on a beach, white sand,
and that night at the casino on Front Street,
the Casino Rouge et Noir,
money spilled through your fingers
onto the green felt of the gambling table.
I remember moving my hand along your thigh.

We didn't speak of it:
how you drew in your breath at the hand dealt,
how girls in green velvet pushed up their breasts,
how even my courtings fell to dust before your blind eye.

Outside in the *steegjes*
counting all our losses but one,
I felt the dangerous lure of the ocean at night.
That beach was beautiful.
But in my dream, a deck of cards,
one fluttering to the ground, blank.
A voice that warned: *Here, this is for you.*

A Tour on an Early Visit to a Tropical Island

A truck rusting by the side of the road.
Shattered beer glasses. Shacks of corrugated tin.

The tour had started like any other:

An open-air bus, cameras clicking, tropical rainforests,
native birds, green fields in a checkerboard.

At the plantation, we watched women pick glossy red fruits
from low bushes with oval leaves and put them in baskets.

We were near Naranjo, where each year a festival
honors the Virgin of Lourdes—
comforter of the afflicted, who knows our wants—
who appeared in white, in dazzling light, in a cave.

"These beans are the best in the world," our guide said.

Later when I read what the women earn
for every basket they fill, and remembered what I pay
for one cup of coffee, I wondered:
How do we live in this world?

The world is always skewed, so much hidden.
Even when the Virgin Mary appeared to Bernadette
in that dark grotto, she promised to make the girl happy,
not in this world, but the next.

Chez Daisy

This is as good as it gets:
here, on the bay at Grand Case
on a stone-paved balcony
above jade-blue water.
There's a white linen cloth, wine in stemmed glasses.
Across the table, my husband.
My son's head in my lap.
When Jonathan wakes, he dangles his feet
over the water below
while we eat lobster bisque,
Caesar salad, conch.

Some things have changed since last year:
There's a new owner but the same clear view
of Saba, where we mounted steps
of volcanic rock through
climbing bougainvillea
and blue-bird hibiscus.

Where we sit now, eating Chez Daisy
in the Windward Islands,
there is time for everything,
and everything is in its place:
sunlight winking on glass and silver,
the pressing weight of the white cloth,
the brush of a *passaat* wind,
and water, lapping at the shore,
silent as time's passage,
so even those who look
don't see what's borne away.

First Winter

Cold reached in
through century-old walls
pushing us toward one
fierce, small fire of faith,
feeding the flames
that whispered, *God is here.*

Behind walls of purple,
that highest color,
we watched snow bury
the particulars of Adams Street.
It left our bushes burdened.
Rhododendrons and mountain laurel
stood waxen and voiceless.
The firs kept to themselves,
knowing no one.

Can you imagine
how much I desired
a first sign of spring that year,
with its hint of resurrection?
It is now that we most desire.

Etruscan Tomb Paintings

I

I remember the clement afternoon
we entered the Tomb of the Bulls,
remember its double-sloped ceiling
and gaily-painted bands of lozenges and circles.
On a terracotta painting, we saw
Iphigenia, armless, being carried
by a winged creature to her death.

That year, I turned to your face
above all others, tracing
the long line of your brow,
dropping the cloak of desire over your head.

It was Iphigenia
her father chose to sacrifice
so he could enjoy fair winds
to pilot his ships to Troy.
Now Iphigenia, with long painted brow
and cryptic smile,
looks up toward the man
who holds her without regard
as a white-tuniced Apollo
leads Iphigenia and her winged captor.

Massive, with muscular legs,
the men are ruddy and full-featured
while Iphigenia's profile lies colorless
on a light-toned ground.
Apollo is armed with bow and arrow.

That year, in love, I too was eager to
accompany archers, angels, gods.
But too often the god visits,
wounds with his arrows, departs.

Still, beyond this terracotta slab,
Iphigenia is saved from the altar.
Artemis, virgin huntress
and goddess of the white moon,
rescues, leaving a stag in her place.

II

Even in a small reproduction
at Tomb of the Baron
you can face a woman's mysteries,
accept death, or an impression of it,
like this cloak the color of pomegranate seeds
being laid on her pale shoulders.

You can see the boy and man
offer the woman a cup of animating wine.
Her arms welcome them,
and for a time you imagine,
her cape drops.

Some long-ago painter
framed their brief lives in vines
to record a ritual
we all must undergo.

For now, though,
let us still be betrayed
by intoxicating kisses
and, in the bacchanalia
of daily life, forget the cup will empty.

III

Two heraldic beasts
guard the entrance
to the Tomb of the Bulls.
Curious and potent,
they gaze past the sign of Venus:
a sphere topped by a small cross.

Here, in figures painted
by gloomy Etruscans,
male meets female
in a heady rush,
their edges suggestive,
contours blurred.

Hands too large,
fingers too long,
these limestone figures
render their duty, say:
remember your death.

IV

Unarmed, on horseback, Troilus approaches
a well-head on which lie two black-faced beasts:
lions with queer ebony faces.
Near a palm tree, Achilles advances
in helmet and shin-greaves, brandishing his sword.

These painted figures speak of the instant before ambush,
when virtue is a cloak draped across shoulders
and imagination is inexhaustible.
In images scratched on stucco, words

are made flesh, the future always one hoofbeat ahead.
There, blood will flow, and Cressida desert Troilus
for a Greek. But it is this one instant art must ambush:
in fresh mineral paint or tensile words
the fronds, lozenges, and stylized pomegranates,
the bird perched momentarily on a limb.

Watchman of the Night

An insomniac, he feels night's muzzle tighten
as he sits on the porch under one bare bulb
like a close moon.

Soon, someone signs his name in a foreign tongue
while crickets, elusive as lost eyelashes or Andalusian gypsies,
chirr in the country beyond the porch.

Bruised by near shadows,
he decides to stuff his guilt once and for all
into the o-shaped mouths of blossoms.
But he's still awake an hour later
and watches a sad-faced rabbit bed in jungle grass,
rediscovers that mounds of ivy breathe.

As the moon glints off the birdbath
and dogs howl two doors down
he watches his wife inside the house
lift her hand to the phone before it rings.

Finally he burrows in bed beside her,
listens—this time for the sound
of fences coming down.

Family Argument, Dawn Beach

A single brown leaf
bends to beach grass
like the wife to her book
or their child to the mysteries
of sand crabs.
Behind them, a leaf stares
with one bug-eaten eye,
mocking such postcard happiness,
while seaweed stretches
to an ocean just out of reach:
just as their love falls short
before the boy's clear eye.

Shadows blacken faces;
salt-bitten words sting.
When they finally touch,
their eyes don't meet.
Husband and wife look down
to footprints in the sand
from other fights and other losses
in a pattern only they can see.

Travelling on Business as a New Mother

Another woman's baby floats
in a chair like a tiny bibelot.
This hotel could be anywhere:
near a plaza, the Alameda,
a place where people
know what they're doing.
The baby smiles like a seated Buddha.
Tall, unfamiliar spirits
migrate past. The fabric
is Brunschwig and Fils.

What brought me here?
Work, that cab, a claustrophobic flight.
The wind blew so hard
I could not hear.
The views changed so often
I could not see.
Is this hotel where I've been heading?
Even at night, in my dreams?

The baby smiles in front of me,
and I consider all I have missed.

King Kong

Kong was never intended to be anything but the best damned adventure film ever made, which it is; and that's all it is.
—Merian C. Cooper, screenwriter

What happens
when the big, awkward ape of wishing
breaks through the Hall of Mirrors
and stands *plop* in front of you
in all his drudgery: missing button,
frayed collar, shadows under the eyes.

You're shorter than when I met you.
Less hair. Fatter stomach.
But boy, your tongue and finger
still know how to make me sing!

Fear is contagious.
I can't tell in which of us
it starts, ricocheting off skin,
mirrors, the pearly membrane of bubbles.

What a lovely mess it would be,
if our big old dream
—of you and me—
stayed true. Splattered bubble juice,
broken mirrors. Someone might get hurt.

But who's the one
who'll make the monkey move?
I'd welcome you.
I'd bring out my courage,
shine its silvered surface until it smokes.
No more hiding behind black glass for me.
No more skulking in shadows or jungle grass.

This marriage has been
a model of slow motion animation.
I want it to move, damn it, move.

Nantucket

Flying from Bread Loaf to 'Sconset
that long-ago summer, my luggage was lost—
diverted elsewhere by some man's hand.

In Vermont I came *this close* to
leaving my present life. Ready
to jump toward an invisible shore,
not knowing if the rocks
would afford footing,
or even abound with startling riches: starfish,
seaweed, littlenecks, and cherrystones.

I dreamt of breaking down houses,
felt the sun stab my skin, searched
the dim, cool interior of my heart.
In front of me,
my infant daughter slept in shade
while roses clambered
up grey-shingled walls.
I heard the throbbing of distant surf,
saw my daughter's toes escape her sandals.

Nantucket! Melville wrote, *Take out your map
and look at it. See what a real corner
of the world it occupies; how it stands there
away off shore, all beach without a background.*

And there were the roses! Coral Tropicana,
Golden Shower, Red Blaze, White Dawn.
Intricate trellises supporting them
like the tiresome, sheltering edifice
of family, diverting their stems

from winding under woodwork
where blossoms will wilt
without enough sun.

Even His Red Heart

If I launch a thread toward him
it will pull me to the hinterlands,
into the place of green-jeweled towers.

Once when I looked into my husband's eyes,
I saw my real self,
or no self,
in a pool of recurring reflections.

Now, if I cast a baited line
through the gill of his eye,
he might imagine pain for an instant
crossing the well-protected border
of his mind. After that, it would be different:

wind blowing through his chest
until even his red heart
glows transparent in my hand.

Cover-Ups

He never listened when I said Price Club
was the best thing since sliced bread
though they had 4-loaf bags and my best first purchase
was a lifetime supply of White-Out which dried up
before he bought me that IBM Selectric typewriter
for our second anniversary and later, after we'd moved
to another state both geographically and metaphorically,
he "discovered" Costco and fell in love on his own.

He never listened when I said George Bush Jr.
was just trying to finish what his father had started
and we really shouldn't go over there,
I said, but he drowned me out, saying
the President must know what to do
and besides he, my husband, worked
for a pharmaceutical company now
and was obligated to donate to the Republican Party
though I thought he'd been a liberal when we met
and later, he couldn't admit he'd been wrong
about what the President knew and didn't know,
or much of anything really.

He never listened when I said,
everybody's fighting wars,
and everybody's wounded, even you,
but by that time neither of us could hear
a word the other said though all of them,
even the angry ones, covered over other words,
like *love me, I need you. Listen, please listen.*

Deep Bottom Pond, West Tisbury

The fog stockpiles
in a bowl of scrub oak and swamp azalea.
I never knew why you left.
I sat for days until I spied your face
in the water. But this summer
I cannot rise to the surface.
Even the trivial weight
of the fog presses me down.

The Year I Didn't Listen to Music

Even harmony would have hurt.
I couldn't risk feeling anything after you left.
Sound molecules like a *sortie*,
an intrusion, felt armed and dangerous.
So the house was kept quiet
like my childhood home,
where no music charged the air
and no pictures touched the walls.

The year I stopped listening to music,
I understood how someone could feel
so fragile—
that the more they could do
to keep the outside out, the better.
Because art penetrates. Music changes the heart.

Paintings and photographs draw
the eyes up until it's like standing on tiptoe,
the way my mother might have done,
peering over the wooden railings of a fence,
surrounded by the sweet, sweet smell
of horses and hay, until an afternoon
when everything stopped:

The barn door closed,
tearing off slats of sunlight,
leaving only ancient silent mysteries
I could never understand.

Noise or Quiet, Which Do You Prefer?

He said this felt like the real holiday to him,
away from the clamoring family.
I knew what he meant,
remembered vacation days with the man
who used to be my husband
barking into a cell phone
about lawsuits and pharmaceuticals
and the boy and girl in the backseat
sparring their own youthful litigation,
all those voices filling my head.

I told the third floor women
I wanted to be half there,
half somewhere else
then found myself alone,
in silence.

So I said to him, *Don't knock it;*
I miss feeling trapped.
The grass is always striated,
never greener.
Justice isn't anywhere we look
for something other than what we have,
and the only real argument
clamors inside.

Hospital

I know it's a cliché but I can't help thinking it.
Twenty-five years now. I sympathized
with the woman scrubbing the floor at the hospital.
Somehow I knew you'd left her to clean up the mess.

Last night in dreams I saw
women you'd made love to.
We exchanged stories.
I watched you bow your head in disgrace
then quickly re-assume that lawyerly pose.

My clothes were packed and ready to go.
My daughter asked if that was the room
where I met the man I fell in love with.
I wasn't doing well at my job,
half of me always leaning toward you.
And you, of course, nowhere to be found.

I thought you loved me.
I don't know why any of us refuse
the love we're given.

Last night in those dreams,
I drove an ambulance to the hospital
to pick up an old man
even though you'd told me not to.

I was the one driving.
And you were the old man
in the ambulance, dying for love.

Sometimes You Sense the Difference

When you stare at the eggs' pale shells,
you remember violets
leaning against the side of a porcelain cup,
their stems in still water,
their purple-cloved heads
royal against the white rim.

We witnessed their struggle among bricks,
breaking through those ruddy jailers.

I remember a fistful of violets
and rain on my lips,
our two-step of pressing and releasing.

These are smoke memories only.
Now everything's locked
in finger-smudged photographs,
hidden in stairwells,
gesturing from a shadowy door
on a crowded street, in midday,
like a dangerous stranger panhandling for trust.
You walk on, your hat low,
your umbrella pointed purposefully before you.

On Hearing a Widow Speak

She said she felt like Emily Dickinson without the poetry,
never getting out of bed but once

on the anniversary of her mother's death.
I told you, knowing you would remember

the book her husband wrote, the one about the way
we mark time and the light that saves us.

With a TV thrown in, literally, for good measure.
I think I've spent my whole life missing someone.

Now even take-out Chinese tastes
like I should be eating it with you.

III This Meditation

*If we know the divine art of concentration,
if we know the divine art of meditation,
if we know the divine art of contemplation,
easily and consciously we can unite
the inner world and the outer world.*

—Sri Chinmoy

Birth

Where's that man I once dreamed of?
A figure swimming inside my frame.
I would will him beyond the cage of my bones
so he could stand before me, smile.

Here I am, his eyes would whisper.
You knew all along I would be here.
Was here. Will be.

He wears a plaid flannel shirt,
soft blue jeans, a brown belt.
He has dark hair.

I will not yell at you, he promises.
I will not let you down.
I will put my hands on your shoulders.
I will slip them inside your blouse.
My tongue will meet yours;

a current will run between us.
All of Life is in that current.
Everything you have ever known and more.
It is the same river that made me inside you
and you inside me.
It is time for us to find each other.

I pry open my rib cage,
let my heart breathe his coming.

I feel him begin
to slip into the world.
I pull my ribs apart farther,

farther. It doesn't hurt.
Faceless, formless,
he slides into *this*.

The Frog King

This is one way the adventure begins:
someone blunders, a golden ball drops,
water ripples in a brick-ringed pool.
From deep springs under a linden tree,
a knobby head emerges to see the bare-footed
woodlander. The frog lifts his eyes to stare
at the straw-haired maiden in newsprint.
Ugly, ugly, she cries, *and not for me.*

Do you want the ball? the puddlesplasher asks.
Just promise me I can sit at your table,
eat off your plate, lie in your bed.

Missing her shiny bauble, she says: *Fine.*
He dives, finds the pretty toy,
and throws it in maidengrass.
The devious princess runs to her father's court.
Then comes something crawling—*splash, splash*—
up the marble stair. A knock, she opens the door,
closes it quickly. It's him. But Daddy holds her

to her promise: makes her take the waterplopper
to table, where he eats heartily, and to bed.
Picking him up by two fingers, she throws him
against a wall, hard. *There, you nasty frog!*
But then he becomes a prince
with affable eyes and seductive lips.

So imagine this:
an incident as small as a dropped ball,
an accident really, that leads to kismet.
You already have most of what you need:

Every daddy is a king. The tree:
any mid-point between dark and light.
A gold (meaning immortal) sphere (meaning perfection),
a soul to toss around. And then the luminous well,
where wishes are still answered.

Later that winter, walking hand in moist hand
with her love, what did the princess find
but ripe, red strawberries under the snow.

Orphanage at St. John the Baptist's Retreat Center

Maybe once the leaves have dropped,
the voices are easier to hear,
those informal prayers of motherless children
and childless women.

One night in December, while you slept,
the long-ago orphans roamed the halls,
quietly turning doorknobs,
tiptoeing into small cubicles
they once called home
though home was a moving target
and neither Santa Claus nor Jesus
could ever really find them
though the sisters of the convent
beseeched the gray skies,
their asexual wails snaking
through naked branches
while cold breaths, unsourced,
pressed against the window panes
and inside, so many hearts
burned and burned and burned,
more dazzling than any votive candles,
a bonfire of solitudes,
each flame longing to merge
with the heartrending brightness of others.

What's Inside That's Always Missing

St. Augustine called it the god-shaped void
and Rumi called it longing
and yes it's the answer to the question
Why are you always grieving?

Sometimes I think
too much about this
and wonder
why everyone else doesn't.

This morning the dream image
of a man climbing out of a hole.

This morning soft snores
but they were from the other side of the wall.
Sleeping alone for so long,
I barely remember what's missing.
But when I step to the low-hung mirror,
I see I've grown far past childhood,
when I bought penny candy
at the corner store
in Burlington, Iowa:
red wax lips and Lik m Aid,
candy buttons on strips of paper.
Chocolate cigarettes that gave
way to the real thing in college,
then pitchers of beer and
squares of Yellow Sunshine
and Faulkner, Melville,
sex on waterbeds.

And with everything that went into my mouth
and everything that went into my heart
I was searching, even later that morning with the poets,
sounding the silence before they named what they'd seen.

Remembering Mark Strand

When I think of Mark Strand
I remember his eyes meeting mine,
or so I imagined, as he spoke at
Bread Loaf and urged me to
"put on those shoes and run,"
telling me, really, to write,
or so I imagined, because I'd
gone running each morning on the hills
around Ripton, and wanted
to write, or maybe even more
wanted someone to tell me to write
and there he was, tall
and impossibly handsome,
doing just that.

When I think of Mark Strand
I remember sitting with Jim Kilgo
on those creamy yellow Adirondack chairs,
our feet bare in the grass, talking about
the way writers, at least literary writers,
write for each other, and about M. Scott Peck's
book *The People of the Lie*, which I'd been
reading on the plane from Burlington, Vermont,
and which started a multi-year conversation
with Jim, who, like Mark, is now gone.

I remember Peck's story about the boy
whose parents gave him for Christmas
the same rifle his brother had used
to kill himself the year before
and how Peck called them evil.

I am glad Mark Strand and Jim Kilgo
were in this world, and wrote of this world,
and how so much of everything we need to know
is already inside us, and the dark cave of the world
is always waiting to be lit.

On Her Father's Boat

An image persists of a tawny girl
on her father's fishing boat at fourteen:
her cinnamon face brushed with dawn,
her eyes berry-brown and credulous.
Her legs scramble among good omens on the deck.
Under poppy-tiled roofs, windows weep herbs
while snow-capped Mt. Athos towers above the Aegean,
harsh monasteries clinging to its cliffs.

Banned to females, this rock can be reached
only by men, on ropes and knotted ladders,
so these things the girl will never see:
St. Nicholas of the Oyster,
a cloth dropped by Mary at Calgary,
fragments of the True Cross.
In caves and Spartan huts
the monks live with their prayers:
kissing icons, snuffing candles.
Bones of brother monks pile high
in the charnel house
near a piece of Christ's crown.

Still, the reach of men runs only so far:
the girl may yet have other possibilities.
For now, as sunlight flecks the waves,
she watches her father's water-whitened fingers
move deftly over his stubborn nets,
untangling the hours.

La Sécheresse

One woman, one tree.
    —Anonymous

When Senegalese women
tend their communal garden,
they water vegetables
from a hand-dug well
one bucket at a time.
Their *animatrice,* or leader,
has seven children
but only half a harvest.
As she bends dry dun hands
to cracked ground, the Harmattan wind
peels topsoil and carries
her continent's cast-off skin
many kilometers south.

When she gives the women buckets
to water the soil,
plant the trees,
feed the children,
they draw a garden—
full, green, and fertile—
from parched earth.

The animatrice, blowing life
into her disciples,
reminds them their tribe has a riddle:

Where does the dry season go in rainy season,
and where does the rainy season go in dry?

When they are silent,
she answers for them:

Into the acacia tree
evergreen, with pendulous leaves
and silver wattle.

It's from you, she insists,
dusting her pinched breasts,
the tree comes; even to him—our tribe's chief—
the tree remains a riddle.

This Meditation

On the oval leaves of the azalea bush,
their edges curl so each one becomes a cup,
a prayer, ready to receive.
On the tufted titmouse skittering inside those branches,
looking for all the world as though all the world
is a leafy, verdant playground.
On the wind chime hanging from the rafter,
its five thin copper tubes like fingers,
reaching, shimmering in the whisper of a wind, silent.

Beyond all this, a hill slopes,
dry leaves and fallen branches
form the visual field's coat
of one color, brown, in all its variations.
Tulip poplars, red oak rise to sky.

I could go on: meditating on the flat stones laid as a low wall,
the moss green bird feeder, a tower of well-seasoned wood
chopped after last year's storm.
All this and more within the frame of my window!

Outside the frame, books on shelves, rows
of signatures, cities, dates. A leather chair.
A slice of lemon floating in water.

Even further, through a different kind of sight,
I see my dog sleep on the couch in the room behind me,
happy in the silence of dreams.

Waiting

Beyond the window
white dogwood blossoms wail.
There *is* grace in this world.
I think of our last look before we parted,
the penetration into woods
untrod since your last stay.

The flowering that takes place
when you arrive. I didn't expect it:
this benediction of blossoms.
Their brief beauty hangs exposed;
is it too late?

On pleasure and pain's
twin branches, white
becomes more than mere background.
Maybe this is the way to live.
So it's desire that really counts,
that answers what's deep inside my woods.
Leaving the rest only a show—
some passing marvel of white.

Small News Item after 9/11

It's hard to talk about benefiting from human tragedy
but The Cotton Ball, a fabric and home décor store
in Morro Bay, California, enjoyed sales
one-third above normal that day.
Within hours of the attacks, women streamed in, nestling
into purple chenille-covered sofas, cradling mugs of coffee,
buying red, white, and blue fabric for flags,
and $1500 Bererra sewing machines.

Months later, Valley sews an 8 x 8 square for a quilt.
On it, there's a tree. White birds feather its branches.
A circle of children rings the brown 100% cotton trunk.

You Asked What Sustains Me

In the movie *Night of the Iguana*
a young Richard Burton
asks Deborah Kerr
what the spooks of depression respect.

Endurance, she says.

In that same movie, Ava Gardner
survives on rum and coke,
and her midnight swims in the ocean
with eager young men.

An old man recites
his last poem
before a white moon
veiled by clouds
that hang soft above
deep, dark water.

Staring at a Painting in a Hospital Where
My Friend is Having Surgery

In the painting,
far away from your resolute doctors
and kind nurses in hospital blues,
yellow wishbones fall from a flawless sky.
I think: *Wish you may, wish you might.*

If only healing could be instant:
a wish easily fulfilled with one pure look
at those cobalt crosses, painted in thick impasto.

Van Gogh said cobalt was a divine color:
"there is nothing as fine
for putting an atmosphere round things."
He painted rapidly, with urgency,
using just what he saw before him.

"You couldn't remember everything,"
the doctor said later. But I remember
the sunflower starbursts.

Between Seasons

You think of the moment
between the asking and the answer.

That spasm of celebration
when your drink arrives
and you glance out the window to see

a boy and his sneakers
quizzing the outer ledge of the bridge.
Three friends sprout from the sidewalk.
Below, a creek shrinks to a thin line.
Near the boy's head
branches ache to cradle him.
His friends wear giddy smiles,
tiny perfect images of the sun
caught in each eye.

Further on, the creek
becomes a river,
frozen silver and radiant
with sun-tossed coins.

Now, before the fall
that may or may not happen,
the tree on the bank
stands black, bare, wary.

Aurora

Even when we saw
the Northern Lights
we kept talking.
Curls of smoke,
the dog-tail ends
of sentences rose,
curved with the wind
under our jackets.
The sky a high ebony
pastry board, flour-dusted.
The lights came so quickly,
we kept talking,
our words mere cookie cutters,
trying to give form to loves
we'd lost, trivial
beneath the larger hands
that shape us.

Conversation

God is the electricity that surges between us.
　　　　　　　　　　　—Martin Buber

Once I spoke to a dozen Chinese executives
who didn't understand English.

My words floated
between us stupidly.
I felt like a puppet,
filling hours and air,
with nothing, with anything,
as long as it occupied
the space between us.

One night I dreamt
of a room full of people
reading their parts
from a script that would change their brains
the way dual-hemisphere meditation,
surgery, and the end of a love affair do.

I want so much to communicate.
I want so much for my words
to be heard.

Ripe fruit plucked from the space
between us and eaten like peaches,
their juice nourishing your chin.

Trapeze

Dark woman in a white dress
sits atop a waterfall,
woods and rocks behind her
in the black and white photo.
Even the act of sitting is a cascade.

When Nic Wallenda crossed Niagara Falls
his shirt shone bright red against the black sky
and the water's turbulent white.
That long, graceful curve of his pole—
it takes so little to find your balance.

Even if noisy thoughts surge between you
and the still silence of that photo,
remember that fear can be contained,
perhaps even loved. With luck,
something unseen keeps you aloft.

The Yellow Brick Road

has an end I hadn't
noticed before now.
I've worn out so many pairs
of shoes, some red, some stained
with juice in the shape of an unknown continent.
Travelling always from home
to what, at the time, looked like elsewhere.

Skipping back and forth—
peering into the refrigerator of a Midwestern childhood,
searching for hugs, or scavenging the secrets
behind green velvet drapes.
What would I have done without the longest loves of all,
or a beloved dog at my side?

I would say this year is a milestone
but which one isn't? Which day less
story-filled than any other?
No wonder the road was the color of fear.
It's what kept me going for such a long time.
Hoping, always hoping, the next wizard
would be real, the screaming monkey mind grow silent

The yellow brick only seems to go from here to there.
Once you've travelled it enough times you know
even the road is as fake as the Great Oz himself.
Providing only the image of motion.
The road really does stop here.

I spin in dizzy, glorious circles,
the blue-and-white checked skirt
swirling around my knees in a wider and wider

flurry, making its presence felt in the only world
the road led to.

Imagine one brick, bounded on all sides.
Large enough for two dazzling red shoes to land on.
Then, dance as though your life depended on it
because it does.

Imagine circles not lines
and violets blooming impossibly high
around you.

Imagine fear turning into sunshine
and concealing green drapes melting into a heap.
The witch, the broomstick, the lion, the scarecrow, the tin man
all characters in a play, even the dog in the basket.
Auntie Em only standing in for love waiting for you at home.
Picture the garden. The mountain. The guards.
All of it a global dream.
What if we knew it was one dream we all shared?
What if we finally woke up?
Imagine no distance between here and there.
The moment of the big bang, your life
no bigger or less important than that.

About the Author

Donna is the author of The Silver Baron's Wife (PEN/New England Discovery Award, Bronze winner in Foreword reviews 2017 Book of the Year Award, Will Rogers Medallion Award and Paterson Prize for Fiction Finalist, more), Sympathetic People (Iowa Fiction Award Finalist and 2015 Next Generation Indie Book Awards Finalist in Short Fiction), and Sometimes You Sense the Difference (Finishing Line Press chapbook). She was a Founding Editor of Bellevue Literary Review and founded and publishes Tiferet Journal. She has received a Bread Loaf Scholarship, Johns Hopkins University MFA Fellowship, grants from the New Jersey Council on the Arts and Poetry Society of Virginia, a Scholarship from the Summer Literary Seminars, and more.

Donna's poems and stories have appeared in Virginia Quarterly Review, Confrontation, Prairie Schooner, New York Quarterly, Washingtonian, New Ohio Review, Ascent, Puerto del Sol, and many other journals as well as in the anthologies I've Always Meant to Tell You (Pocket Books), To Fathers: What I've Never Said (featured in O Magazine), Men and Women: Together and Alone from Spirit That Moves Us Press.